Violin

SCHIRMER'S LIBRARY
OF MUSICAL CLASSICS

FRIEDRICH SEITZ

Pupil's Concertos

For Violin and Piano

ISBN 978-0-7935-5238-2

G. SCHIRMER, Inc.

DISTRIBUTED BY

HAL•LEONARD®
CORPORATION
7777 W. BLUEMOUND RD. P.O. BOX 13819 MILWAUKEE, WI 53213

Fourth Pupil's Concerto

for
Violin

Edited and fingered by
Philipp Mittell

Friedrich Seitz. Op. 15

20689

Meno mosso

Tempo I

Grandioso

Andante con moto

20689

Fourth Pupil's Concerto

Edited and fingered by
Philipp Mittell

Violin

Friedrich Seitz. Op. 15

20689

4

Violin

Andante con moto

20689

Violin

20689